RAND McNALLY

Oceans & Seas

A *Where Are We?* Book

by Chris Arvetis
and Carole Palmer
illustrated by James and Doris Buckley

Rand McNally
for Kids™
Books•Maps•Atlases

Oceanographers use research ships, submarines, satellites, and computers to learn about the oceans. They study what the ocean bottom looks like and how it was formed. Oceanographers also study the ocean plants and animals.

Water from each ocean joins to form one big *world* ocean. The ocean is the home of the world's largest animal, the blue whale. It can be over 100 feet long and weigh 150 tons.

Whales are mammals. They breathe with lungs. They must return to the surface to breathe at least every 40 minutes. The whale surfaces, breathes, and dives in one continuous motion, taking less than two seconds to breathe.

The *Atlantic* and the *Indian* oceans are the next largest ones. The *Arctic Ocean* is the smallest one. It is by the North Pole and is covered by ice most of the time.

Brrr!

Two well-known animals that live in the ocean are dolphins and sharks. Dolphins are mammals and are very intelligent. They can be trained to perform in water shows. Dolphins are 4 to 30 feet long and weigh from 100 pounds to 5 tons.

Sharks belong to one of three groups of fishes. They can be 40 feet long and weigh over 15 tons. Their streamlined bodies allow them to move very rapidly. Many sharks have mouths on the underside of the head and several rows of teeth. New teeth grow every one to two weeks.

Oceans have smaller bodies of water called *seas*.
Oceans seas are partially surrounded by land.
Oceanographers have identified over 50 seas.

Timor Sea

Coral Sea

Indian
Ocean

AUSTRALIA

Pacific
Ocean

Tasman
Sea

TASMANIA

NEW
ZEALAND

N
↑

Smaller parts of the oceans are called seas.
The Mediterranean and Caribbean are seas in the Atlantic Ocean.
Oceans can also have areas called gulfs.
The Gulf of Mexico and the Persian Gulf are two well-known gulfs.
Bays are also part of an ocean.
The Bay of Bengal is in the Indian Ocean.

Gulfs are large areas of oceans partly surrounded by curved coastlines. *Bays* are usually smaller than gulfs.

N

UNITED STATES

Pacific Ocean

MEXICO

Gulf of Mexico

Atlantic Ocean

CUBA

Oceans have salt water.
Ponds and lakes have fresh water.
Salt water tastes just like fresh water with salt sprinkled in it.
Rivers, volcanoes, and underwater springs bring the salt to the ocean.
As the fresh water evaporates, the salts are left.
The hotter the climate, the saltier the ocean.

Not too much.

Ocean water is 96% hydrogen and oxygen. The other 4% is composed of 85 other elements, mostly salts. *Salinity* is the term used to describe the amount of salt in the ocean water.

Water 96.5%

Salts 3.5%

As the sun shines on the water, the ocean often looks blue. Some areas along the coast look green because of the plants. Parts of the Red Sea look red because of the heavy red algae growth. The Yellow Sea carries mud that makes it look yellow.

This must be the shoreline.

You are standing on dry land now. Large land areas on the earth are called *continents*.
The *shoreline* is where the land and water meet.
As we go into the ocean, we first find the *continental shelf*.
It is underwater land that slopes down from the shoreline.

A *continental margin* is the term for the section from the shoreline to the ocean floor. The continental margin includes the continental shelf, the continental slope, and the continental rise.

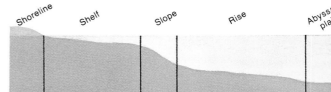

Shoreline Shelf Slope Rise Abyssal plain

The continental shelf along the eastern coast is wide because the land slopes gently into the Atlantic Ocean. The continental shelf along the western United States is narrower because the mountainous land drops into the Pacific Ocean.

At the end of the continental shelf, the land drops off.
This is the *continental slope*.
Here the ocean becomes much deeper.
Then we reach very deep water on the ocean floor.
The ocean floor has many features.
There are large flat areas called *abyssal plains*.
That's a big term!

Coral reefs are found on the continental shelf in the warm waters of the South Pacific Ocean and the Caribbean Sea. There are three main types of coral reefs.

1 *Fringing reefs* touch the shoreline of a volcanic island.

2 *Barrier reefs* are separated from the volcanic island by a lagoon. The Great Barrier Reef of Australia is a very large barrier reef (1250 miles long).

Lagoon

3 An *atoll* is found farther out in the ocean and is a ring of coral reefs. The volcanic island it surrounds has sunk into the ocean.

There are thousands of underwater mountains called *seamounts*.
A seamount has steep sides and a small peak.
Some seamounts stick out of the surface of the water and form islands like the Hawaiian Islands.
A seamount that has a flat top is called a *guyot*.

If it's flat on top, it is a guyot.

Oceanographers have found over 1000 *seamounts*. The Pacific Ocean has more than either the Atlantic or the Indian Oceans. The Loihi Seamount in the Hawaiian Islands is underwater and is slowly growing taller. Scientists predict that it will eventually become another island.

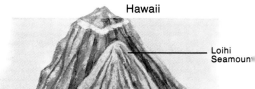

Hawaii

Loihi Seamoun

The island of Hawaii is the top of a very large volcano. It is the highest mountain on the earth when measured from its bottom on the ocean floor to its peak. It is over 31,000 feet tall.

31,000 ft

The ocean floor also has *trenches*. Trenches are long, narrow cracks in the ocean floor.
The deepest trench is in the Pacific Ocean and is called the Mariana Trench.
The deepest spot in the trench is called the Challenger Deep. It is over 36,000 feet deep.

The deepest part of the oceans are the trenches along the edges of the ocean floor. The length and the depth of the trenches make them remarkable ocean structures. At these depths, the cold temperature, water pressure, and lack of light make difficult living conditions. There are no plants, but animals like the sea cucumbers, worms, clams, and glass sponges can be found.

The chart shows the major ocean trenches in the Pacific, Atlantic, and Indian Oceans.

Trench

Pacific Ocean		Atlantic Ocean		Indian Ocean	
Trench	Feet	Trench	Feet	Trench	Feet
Marina	36,195	Puerto Rico	28,374	Java	25,344
Tonga	35,702	South Sandwich	27,559		
Kurtle	34,586				
Philippine	34,438				

The ocean floor has some of the biggest mountain ranges on earth. The *midocean ridges* are a chain of mountains that run along the ocean floor.

These mountains were made as molten rock escaped through cracks in the ocean floor and piled up to form mountains.

The midocean ridges form a mountain belt from the Arctic Ocean down through the Atlantic Ocean around Africa into the Indian Ocean and across the Pacific Ocean north to North America. Rift valleys are deep crevices in the midocean ridges.

Three fourths of the world's earthquakes occur along the Ring of Fire, an area along the edges of the continents of the Pacific Ocean. Ocean earthquakes can cause giant waves called tsunamis.

Look what I found!

Many plants and animals live in the ocean. There are three main groups of plant and animal life.
One group is called *plankton*.
Plankton are the small plants and animals that float near the surface of the ocean.
Algae and diatoms are plankton.

Plankton are such tiny organisms that a microscope is needed to see them. They float in the water and most cannot move on their own. There are plantlike organisms called *phytoplankton* and animallike ones known as *zooplankton*.

Phytoplankton

Zooplankton

The second group is called *nekton*, which are forms of ocean life that can swim.

Because nekton swim, they can be found near the top of the ocean and on the ocean floor.

Fish, walruses, dolphins, squids, and whales are nekton.

Nekton can move freely throughout the ocean and are good swimmers. The largest group of nekton are fish with over 13,000 kinds. Unusual animals like the squid with 10 arms and octopuses with 8 arms are also nekton.

Octopus

Squid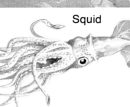

Nekton like whales and porpoises remain in the water all their lives. Others like sea lions, seals, and walruses spend time on land and in the water.

Seals

You have interesting shapes.

We belong to the benthos family.

Benthos live on or near the ocean floor. Some dig into the ocean floor, others attach themselves to the bottom, and still others float around. Kelp and sea grass attach themselves to the bottom. Crabs, clams, lobsters, and starfish live on the ocean floor.

Ray

The third type of ocean life is *benthos*.
Many of these plants and animals grow in shallow ocean waters.
Others live in the deepest part of the ocean.
Starfish, crabs, oysters, barnacles, kelp, and sea grass are benthos.

Interesting ocean birds include the penguins and albatrosses. Penguins spend months at a time out in the ocean. They cannot fly but they are excellent swimmers.

Penguins

Albatross

Ocean water moves all the time.
Wind blowing across the surface
of the ocean creates *waves*.
The size of the waves depends
on the force of the wind and
how long and how far it blows.
Ocean *currents* are like streams or
rivers moving through the ocean.
Currents are caused by the wind.
The currents cause the ocean water
to constantly move in one direction.

Oceans provide many resources. About 200 billion
pounds of fish, which is eaten as food or processed
for fish oil and fish meal, are caught each year.
Seaweeds like kelp are harvested for minerals
and vitamins.

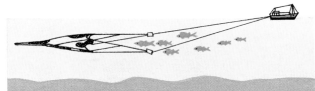

Offshore drilling in the ocean floor brings up oil and natural gas. Minerals are removed from salt water. Medicines are obtained from red algae, marine snails, and horseshoe crabs. Oceans have always been used for transportation and shipping.

As the tides rise and fall, a variety of animals can be found along the ocean shore. Along the rocky shores, mussels secrete a fluid to attach themselves to the rocks. Acorn barnacles have a series of overlapping plates to protect themselves from the pounding waves.

Mussel

Acorn barnacle

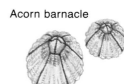

Ocean *tides* are caused by the force of gravity. The tides rise and fall twice each day.

I knew that!

Animals living along sandy shores burrow into the ground for protection from the waves and weather. The cockle can dig into the sand and has two feeding tubes to get water and food. Clams also have a long tube, or siphon, to reach food when they are buried in the sandy beach.

Cockle

Clam

Cruise ships take vacationers to exotic ports around the world. People use oceans for fun and resources. Everyone must work to protect the resources and to keep our oceans free from pollution.